# THE WICCAN BIBLE FOR THE SOLITARY WITCH

*Wiccan Prayers, Beliefs, and Practices*

## By Didi Clarke

D1713756

Disclaimer:
While I have performed all these spells myself, your results may vary.

# CONTENTS

By Didi Clarke

*If you'd like to be notified when I publish a new book or have something exciting in the works, be sure to sign up for my mailing list. You'll receive a **FREE** color magick correspondence chart when you do! Follow this link to subscribe:*

*https://mailchi.mp/01863952b9ff/didi-clarke-mailing-list*

# CHAPTER 1: WALKING THE PATH OF THE SOLITARY WITCH

By nature, we Wiccans are pretty independent people. Most who are drawn to the religion possess an open mind and a strong will—which is a nice combination of personality traits to have, if I do say so myself!

However, taking the "lone wolf" approach to life has its drawbacks too. At times it can feel isolating to blaze your own trail, and learning a new concept or tackling a problem is always easier with friends by your side.

In *The Wiccan Bible for the Solitary Witch*, it's my goal to help you alleviate these two issues while still allowing you to keep the independent, unique spirit that makes practicing magick such an enjoyable, transformative spiritual path!

Are you ready to embrace the way of the solitary witch?

## What Is a Solitary Witch?

Traditionally, witches are part of a coven. This is a group of like-minded people who have been initiated into a particular witchcraft tradition who perform spells and rituals together, celebrate holidays together, and generally just enjoy one another's company.

But joining a coven is not always a possibility or even desirable for some people. Whether distance prevents you from joining one or you simply prefer to journey into the world of spirituality on your own, you are what's known as a solitary witch—someone who practices Wicca or witchcraft by themselves.

This is a perfectly acceptable path to take, and being a solitary witch doesn't make you any less of a full-fledged, practicing Wiccan. In fact, solitary witchcraft has been on the rise since the advent of the internet as more and more people find themselves drawn to the craft but aren't entirely sure where they fit in exactly.

If that sounds familiar, this is the book for you!

# What You'll Find Within These Pages

Like I mentioned just a moment ago, taking this solitary path does come with a few roadblocks. But it's my hope that by the end of this book, you'll find that these two obstacles don't have to hold you back from practicing Wicca.

First, we have the education gap.

Witches who are part of a coven are in some ways at an advantage when it comes to learning the intricacies of witchcraft. They have experienced elders to learn from, who themselves learned from experts—but solitary witches don't have the luxury of generations of accumulated knowledge.

You shouldn't let this hold you back, though! In this book, I'm going to walk you through all the most important concepts that make Wicca the religion that it is. In particular, I'll show you how to become experienced at things like:

- Wiccan Ethics
- Important Wiccan Terms
- How Magick Works
- Wiccan Holidays
- How Wiccans Pray
- Writing Your Own Spells
- Performing Rituals
- And much more!

But what about the camaraderie and support that covens give to witches?

It's important not to underestimate the power of togetherness, but just because you're not part of an official coven doesn't mean you're not part of a group. We solitary witches are linked spiritually each time we sit down to study or practice the craft. We're all part of a universal coven, if you will. With every candle you light, every incantation you recite, know that you have the support and acceptance of solitary witches everywhere!

Are you ready to take this journey with us?

# CHAPTER 2: WICCAN ETHICS AND PHILOSOPHY

B efore we dive into the practice of Wicca, we need to spend a short amount of time discussing the philosophy and ethics that support our religion.

Wicca is a religion that is highly diverse in terms of beliefs and practices. However, despite this (important) diversity, there are a few ethical standards that most, if not all, Wiccans aspire to follow. We don't always live up to these ideals—we're human after all—but these are the things witches believe are necessary for a magickal practice that is responsible, compassionate, and effective.

In this chapter, we're going to be taking a look at the two most important ethical statements within the world of Wicca: the Wiccan Rede and the Threefold Law. For a witch who aspires to be a force for good in the world, these are the guiding principles she lives her life by in order to achieve that.

Unlike some other religions that are preoccupied with obedience and the observance of strict rules, Wicca is a practice of liberation. These ethical guidelines are not meant to feel confining or restrictive—on the contrary, they are here to help you tap into the spiritual power of the universe in the most complete way possible by outlining the karmic laws that govern it.

Additionally, Wiccans must adopt and practice these ethical guidelines of their own free will. We have no angry gods in our religion waiting to punish your each and every misdeed. We take these responsibilities freely upon ourselves without fear of punishment or hope of reward. We follow them for their own sake.

# The Wiccan Rede

"An [if] it harm none, do what ye will."

That right there is known as the Wiccan Rede. It may look and sound deceptively simple, but it is the basis for our entire religion.

For those of you who don't have a passion for ye olde English, the Rede can be rephrased in modern terms like so:

"You are free to do what you want, as long as it doesn't hurt anybody."

For Wiccans, the desire to manifest our own will is of the utmost importance. We're a group of freethinkers that is pretty independent by nature. So, it's no wonder that we've enshrined this desire to blaze our own trail in the most foundational statement of our religion.

However, we still recognize that our actions have consequences and that when we seek to harm others, we deny them the right to live freely—a right that we ourselves so desperately desire. Wiccans believe that all life is sacred and connected, and so to knowingly and intentionally hurt another person simply means that we're hurting ourselves—since we're all united by the divine spirit of the universe.

# The Wiccan Rede in Practice

Faithfully following the Wiccan Rede doesn't have to feel like a precarious balancing act on a tightrope. There's plenty of solid footing to walk this ethical path. But what exactly does it look like in practice?

First and foremost, it means that we don't use magick as a means of revenge or harm.

I'll be the first to admit it—curses, hexes, and black magick are all incredibly real...and incredibly powerful. If you want to do spiritual or physical harm to another person, there is a long list of dark arts you could use to accomplish that goal. But we as Wiccans want to take the high road whenever possible. There is no grudge or grievance that's worth harming another living soul. Because, like I mentioned just above, when we hurt another person, we're merely hurting the universal spirit that connects us all.

Secondly, it means that we don't use magick to influence people against their will and without their knowledge.

Even if you don't mean any harm, using magick to interfere with the free will of other people is frowned upon. How this plays out in real life depends on who you ask, though.

There are some witches who are completely opposed to love spells and love potions because they believe that love is an emotion that shouldn't be manipulated. On the other hand, some Wiccans are perfectly fine with it. We refer to these contentious branches of magick as "gray magick"—since they fall somewhere between white and black.

That being said, every witch has a line that she's not willing to cross, even if that line varies from person to person.

Finally, it means that we don't use animals unethically in our magick.

While animal magick can be incorporated into your practice, Wiccans don't practice animal sacrifice or anything remotely similar to that. We love our furry friends and oppose bloodshed in any form.

As with the free will issue, Wiccans will vary on what counts as ethical when it comes to animals. Some people freely use things like feathers or fur in their magick, while others would find this abhorrent. But we all agree that the taking of a life has no place in the practice of Wicca.

# The Threefold Law

The Threefold Law (or Rule of Three) is a statement about cosmic justice within Wicca. It's not so much a rule to follow as it is a statement about how the energy of the universe works. It's been phrased many different ways, but it ultimately boils down to this:

The energy you put into the world will be returned to you three times over.

So, if you're a source of goodness and light to those around you, you can expect to receive more goodness and light in return. Conversely, if you're intent on spreading misery and sadness, be on the lookout—because it's coming right back at you.

That being said, the Threefold Law is not a math equation. You don't input one good deed and expect precisely three to return to you. Similarly, if you're using magick for evil, you won't necessarily feel those repercussions immediately. The universe doesn't always operate on our schedule, but you can rest assured that it always restores balance to the scales of justice in due time.

# CHAPTER 3: KEY WICCAN TERMS AND SYMBOLS

L ike every religion, Wicca has its own unique terms and symbols, and if you're just getting started, they can be a major stumbling block. In this chapter, I'm going to go over some of the most important and common ones that you'll encounter.

Learning these terms doesn't have to be a chore—you don't have to break out the flash cards and quiz yourself, and I promise there won't be a final test at the end of this chapter. Instead, I find that the best way to understand these major concepts is to encounter them naturally "in the wild." Lots of times, context clues are all you need to help you define an unfamiliar word. However, when you find yourself really stumped, don't hesitate to jump back to this chapter to give yourself a little refresher!

By Didi Clarke

# Wiccan vs. Witch vs. Pagan

Wiccan, witch, and Pagan are quite possibly the three terms you'll encounter most when studying Wicca. And they can be the trickiest too!

Some folks use them interchangeably, and that's perfectly fine—I'm not ashamed to admit that sometimes I do this myself. However, they do have different meanings, and it's important to understand them, even if you don't always get them right 100% of the time.

The term Wiccan is by far the easiest one to nail down: a Wiccan is simply someone who practices the religion of Wicca. This religion was developed by the British occultist Gerald Gardner, and it is a form of witchcraft. However, there are other forms of witchcraft that don't fall under the term "Wicca", so it's important not to make the assumption that all witches are Wiccans.

A witch is a person who is a practitioner of witchcraft. While the definitions of witchcraft can vary between different people and different groups, at its most basic, it's the belief in and practice of any form of magick. So, all Wiccans are witches, but not all witches are Wiccans.

Finally, we come to the term Pagan. This is a term that refers to someone who worships any of the traditional Gods and Goddesses of ancient Europe (before the invasion of Christianity). These include Celtic Gods like Dagda, Morrigan, and Brigid, as well as Norse deities like Odin, Thor, and Freya.

So, if you're a witch or Wiccan that works with these deities, you would also be considered a Pagan. However, if you work exclusively with other deities (Egyptian, African, Chinese, etc.), then you would not technically be considered a Pagan.

Conversely, not all Pagans would be considered Wiccans or witches. These include folks who worship the traditional European Gods and Goddesses but don't practice magick.

# Spell

A spell is any practice that uses magick to harness and use spiritual energy. There are elaborate spells with specific tools and actions (known as rituals), but they can also be as simple as reciting a few lines. Without spells, you don't have Wicca or witchcraft.

And if I'm being perfectly honest, you'll quickly find in this book that I have a tendency to use the terms "spell" and "ritual" interchangeably. Ritual work is by far my favorite type of spellwork, so I often think of them one and the same in my mind!

# Pentagram

The pentagram is the symbol most commonly associated with Wicca. You know it as a five-pointed star enclosed within a circle, and I've got one proudly displayed on the cover of this book.

The four bottom points of the star represent the traditional elements we use within witchcraft—air, fire, earth, and water. The top point of the star represents the divine.

The pentagram is often confused with the pentacle—and many witches prefer this second term because of the association some people have between pentagrams and Satanism. However, if we're being specific, a pentacle is an object (usually a flat disc) that has a magickal symbol inscribed on it. So, all pentagrams are pentacles, but not all pentacles are pentagrams.

# Grimoire/Book of Shadows

A grimoire is any book that contains magickal information—spells, symbols, rituals, and the like. The term Book of Shadows is closely related. It's a grimoire that has been compiled and assembled for personal use by a specific witch.

While using grimoires meant for public consumption (like this book!) is essential to progressing in Wicca, I highly recommend you begin your own personal Book of Shadows, too. Transmitted knowledge is good, but personal experience is invaluable.

# Correspondence

A correspondence is any object or concept that has a magickal association.

Let me take an example from the non-Wiccan world to explain what this means— whether you're a witch or not, the color red frequently corresponds to love or passion.

There are so many things that have magickal correspondences that it would be impossible to list them all, but some common ones include: colors, plants, crystals, days of the week, and planets.

Correspondences are critically important when it comes to creating and performing spells that are powerful and effective. By aligning your tools and practices with their natural energies, you'll find that your magick is much more potent.

# Altar

An altar is where witches and Wiccans perform their magickal work. These can be a permanent fixture in your home or a temporary space that can be put up and taken back down after the end of a ritual.

Designing an altar is one of the most fun and exciting things you can do on your journey into Wicca—it's a place where you can let your own personal style and flair shine through. However, some common items you'll find on most altars include candles, a pentagram, statues of Gods or Goddesses, and your most important magickal tools and books.

# Drawing Down the Moon

Drawing down the Moon is one of the most common and powerful rituals within the world of Wicca. During a full moon, this ceremony is used to invoke the power of the Wiccan Goddess (more on her in a later chapter) and channel her spirit. In covens, this is typically performed by the High Priestess, but solitary witches are free to use this ritual by themselves too.

# Esbat

Speaking of full moons, an esbat is the official celebration or observance of a full moon. Drawing down the Moon obviously fulfills this purpose, but any sort of ceremony or remembrance on a full moon is considered an esbat as well.

By Didi Clarke

# CHAPTER 4: HOW MAGICK WORKS

One of the most common questions about Wicca is this—what makes magick work?

It's perfectly understandable to want to know what the driving force behind magick is, and while this question doesn't necessarily have a clean, straightforward answer, I'm going to do my best in this chapter to explain the thing that gives magick its power.

## Spiritual Energy

Just like everything else in our universe, magick is powered by energy. However, unlike the energy that we get from eating food or the energy our cars get from oil (I'll leave my tree hugger opinions to myself), the energy that powers magick is much more prevalent...and much more ancient.

When we talk about energy in Wicca, we're discussing a concept that has gone by many names throughout human history—qi, prana, God, aether, shatki, spirit, and the list goes on. However, all of these terms point toward the same thing, and that "thing" is energy. This mysterious, formless substance gave rise to the universe and everything that inhabits it. Even though we might not be able to see it with our eyes, it's always there, working behind the scenes to influences our lives—often in ways we don't even realize.

At its most basic, magick is the intentional harnessing and manipulating of this spiritual energy. By performing particular actions, saying particular words, and using particular things, we can (however finitely) tap into this power source to accomplish our will. Magick is not the only way that humans can harness the power of spiritual energy, but for Wiccans, this is the way that feels most comfortable and natural to us.

# Wicca and the Divine

If you think back to the last chapter, you'll remember that a witch is simply someone who believes in and works with magick—they don't necessarily believe in Gods and Goddesses. However, within Wicca you'll find that most practitioners do use the concept of divinity to help them tap into the spiritual energy of the universe.

Because the concept of energy is so nebulous and mind-bending, it can be difficult to connect with it in a meaningful way. And this is why we turn to deities. Gods and Goddesses have attributes, they have personalities, they have likes and dislikes, and they have a history.

In short, they're similar to us.

Personifying spiritual energy in the form of a deity is one way that allows us to wrap our heads around it. There's no way to perfectly define or understand something so all-encompassing, but deities at least allow us a jumping off point into the mysteries of the universe.

For the rest of this chapter, we're going to be taking a look at the principal deities you'll encounter within Wicca.

# The Triple Goddess

The Triple Goddess is our conception of divine feminine power. She is the principal female deity that we worship within Wicca. Additionally, she is closely associated with the changing phases of the moon.

The "triple" part of the Triple Goddess stems from the fact that we conceive of this Goddess as three distinct but closely related representations—the Maiden, the Mother, and the Crone. These three personifications have their own attributes, but when taken as a whole, they add up to the totality of the Triple Goddess. We sometimes invoke a particular aspect of the Goddess, but it's just as common to see us invoking her as the whole, too.

The Maiden represents the Goddess as a vibrant, beautiful young woman. She is a symbol of new life and new beginnings, which is why she is often celebrated in the spring—a time of new life for the entire planet. Additionally, we may turn to the Maiden in particular for blessing or consecration rituals due to her associations with purity. The Maiden corresponds to the waxing (or growing) moon.

Next, we have the Mother. As her title implies, she is associated with motherhood and maternal love. You'll find this aspect of the Goddess is frequently invoked in fertility rituals and when blessing a new child. However, Wiccans of all ages and purposes turn to her when seeking the love and guidance that only a mother can give. The Mother corresponds to the full moon.

Finally, we have the Crone. Even though "crone" might be viewed as a not-very-nice word for an older woman in our culture, old age is a time of respect and great potential within Wicca. A witch reaches the height of her powers as she enters her twilight years. Similarly, the Crone is a source of immense spiritual power, especially concerning psychic abilities. Turn to her to tap into the wisdom of the universe. She corresponds to the waning (or dying) moon.

# The Horned God

As the Triple Goddess is our principal conception of divine feminine power, the Horned God is the principal male deity in Wicca. Typically, he's depicted as a human male with antlers. However, he bears NO associations with the Christian devil—in fact, the Horned God predates the devil by centuries.

The Horned God is a completely benevolent deity, and he represents harmony between humanity and the natural world. As the Triple Goddess is seen as our celestial, lunar mother, he is our father and protector of the earth.

You might hear some witches refer to the Horned God as "Cernunnos." Don't let this confuse you—this is simply the name given to him within the Celtic tradition of witchcraft.

# The Triple Goddess and Horned God as One

Frequently within Wicca, you'll find the Triple Goddess and Horned God invoked as a pair. Sometimes we might simply refer to them as the God and Goddess, but other times, we call them the Lord and Lady of Wicca.

When invoked as one, these two represent the divine unity of spiritual power—they are two sides of the same coin, if you will. Alone or together, they are the divine parents of Wiccans everywhere.

# Other Gods and Goddesses

The more you study Wicca, the more Gods and Goddesses you'll find that we invoke. From Celtic deities to Greek deities to everything in between, there is no shortage of divine figures in witchcraft!

In fact, you'll find that oftentimes we incorporate the deities of other faiths into the archetypes I've described above. For example, when working with the Triple Goddess, some witches prefer to label them as specific ones—like Artemis (the Maiden), Selene (the Mother), and Hecate (the Crone) from Greek mythology.

Working with different groups of Gods and Goddesses (known collectively as a "pantheon"), is a matter of personal preference. I highly encourage you to do some studying on your own and find which manifestations of the divine personally resonate with you.

# CHAPTER 5: WICCAN PRAYERS

Prayer is a form of communication with the spirit world. Even though most people associate Wicca with magick and spells, we actually do a lot of praying too. Although we do sometimes ask for things in our prayers, prayer is more than just begging the universe to give us what we want. It's empowering, comforting, and most importantly, downright magickal!

In this chapter, we're going to be taking a look at how, why, and to whom we pray to in the world of Wicca. I believe that prayer is a great entry point into our religion because of its simplicity. It's free, easy to do, and it brings us closer to the sacred heart of the universe—which is really the whole point of practicing witchcraft.

## Who Do We Pray To?

Like the practitioners of most religions, Wiccans generally pray to our own Gods and Goddesses. Like I mentioned in the last chapter, deities are a personification of spiritual energy, so it makes sense that we would want to start a conversation with them.

Some witches have one or two specific deities that they pray to, while others tailor the targets of their prayers to different Gods or Goddesses depending on the circumstances they find themselves in. I believe that both approaches are perfectly fine, but if you're a complete beginner at praying, I would suggest starting with the

Triple Goddess and the Horned God. These two are very receptive to the prayers of their followers and working with them will give you a solid foundation to expand upon in the future.

However, unlike some other religions, Wiccans can and do pray to beings besides Gods and Goddesses. Some nature-minded witches pray to the earth. Others pray to the spirits of the four elements. We also sometimes pray to our ancestors or other departed figures in our lives. The wisdom and comfort that this approach can bring should not be underestimated.

# Why Do We Pray?

I'll admit it, many of the prayers we make occur when we want something. It might sound selfish at first, but this is a perfectly acceptable practice. This is especially true when the "something" we want is not physical or tangible. We pray for wisdom. We pray for guidance. We pray for comfort. You would be hard-pressed to find someone who would consider those things selfish—they're basic human needs!

However, we can also pray as a form of thanksgiving. If you successfully perform a spell with the help of a God or Goddess, it's customary to offer a small prayer of thanks for their assistance. Wiccan farmers or gardeners might pray to Mother Nature after a good harvest. And after a scare or a close call, you might feel compelled to thank the universe for the simple gift of being alive. As you can see, appreciation is an integral part of praying in Wicca.

Finally, sometimes we pray just to get things off our chests. I don't recommend thinking of deities as your own personal, supernatural therapists, but putting your fear into words or articulating what troubles you can go a long way in improving your state of mind. The spirits of the universe are always willing to lend an ear to someone in distress.

# How Do We Pray?

Honestly, there's not really a wrong way to pray. However, we can classify most prayer into two distinct categories: spontaneous and ritualized.

Spontaneous prayer comes from the heart. You're not reading from a script or reciting memorized lines—you're simply allowing the words to flow out of you as they may. This approach is nice because I think that it gets you comfortable with the act of praying. You're less likely to feel out of your element when the words you're saying feel natural and in your own voice.

However, there are other times when we turn to ritualized, or pre-written, prayers. Sometimes you might feel like you don't know the right words to say, so using a tried-and-true prayer makes sense. Other times you might be praying in a very formal setting or praying about something very serious and solemn. Ritualized prayer can provide the level of respect and reverence you're looking for during these times.

But I want to emphasize again, there's really not a wrong way to pray in Wicca. What's important is that you find a method that works for you and try it out!

In the next section, I'll share some formal prayers for different occasions that you can experiment with.

# Ritual Prayers

Note: I've crafted these using plural first-person nouns like "we" and "us" because I believe they sound more pleasant to the ear and emphasize the interconnected nature of all Wiccans. But it's perfectly fine to replace them with "I" and "me"— this is a book for the solitary witch, after all!

## Prayer at the Birth of Child:

We thank the universe for the gift of life it has given to us. May the great God, our divine father, watch over this child on her/his life journey. And may the loving Goddess, our divine mother, bless her/him with the sacred, radiant light of eternal love.

## General Prayer of Thanksgiving:

All thanks is due to the divine light within us all for the blessings that unfold within our lives. We offer this prayer of gratitude for the riches that have been bestowed upon us. May we always turn our blessings outward, giving more than we receive, to brighten the lives of those around us.

## Prayer for Times of Grief:

Kind Mother of all humanity, we turn to you in our distress. Though our hearts break, we know your divine love can mend them. Though our spirits are crushed, we know your healing power can restore us. And though the path seems dark, we know you continue to guide us and light our way.

## Prayer Before a Trip:

Spirits of the wind, guide us safely to our destination. Bless us with your gentle breeze that our travels may be merry.

## Prayer at the Beginning of a New Day:

Mighty sun, we meet again at the dawn of a new day. Sustain us with your warmth and kindle the fire of life within our hearts that we may greet each new adventure with joy and laughter. As you foster all that is upon our earth, let us foster kindness and peace among all we meet today.

## Prayer at the End of the Day:

Mother moon, watch over us as we sleep. Fill our dreams with the wisdom of the spirits, that we may be drawn closer to you. We thank you for the gift of another day well done and are comforted by the gentle glow of your celestial rays.

By Didi Clarke

## Prayer to Honor the Dead:

The wheel of life turns under the watchful eye of you, oh sacred Crone. We take this time to honor those whose journey has ended before ours, with the knowledge that our path too must one day reach its conclusion. Though they may be gone, we know their spirits are still here with us, guiding us and giving us strength. Bless and protect them as they continue the eternal cycle into higher realms unknown.

# CHAPTER 6: MAJOR WICCAN HOLIDAYS

Although it may sound unexpected, we witches know how to party. Now, you probably won't find many of us doing keg stands or dancing the night away at the club, but the fact remains that we enjoy a good celebration. And that's why we take our holidays so seriously. Sure, holidays may be an important time for special rituals and particular kinds of magick, but at their core, they're about joyfully celebrating the ever-changing, never-ending wheel of life that we all find ourselves a part of.

In this chapter, I'm going to take you through the eight major holidays, or *Sabbats*, that mark the high points on the Wiccan calendar. Each one has its own different flavor and purpose, but they all add up to a yearly celebration of life and spiritual power.

When celebrating the Sabbats yourself, feel free to go all out or use a simple ceremony. You'll probably find yourself drawn to particular holidays based on their origin and purpose, but don't neglect the ones that leave you less-than-excited, either. Each one has its role to play, no matter how small, and as you dig deeper into them, you'll come to see that all holidays are a cause for celebration.

By Didi Clarke

# The Winter Solstice

Also known as Yule or Midwinter, the winter solstice is the official unofficial beginning of the Wiccan year. It's one of the most ancient holidays in all of humankind, for Wiccans and non-Wiccans alike. Researchers speculate that the winter solstice has been celebrated in some form or another since at least the Stone Age!

Astronomically, the winter solstice marks the time of year when nighttime is longest and daytime is the shortest. For those of us who love the long, chilly winter nights, it's doesn't get much better than this.

But Yule is about so much more than this particular point in the earth's journey around the sun. Spiritually, it commemorates the movement from death into rebirth in the cycle of life. Think about it: this is the time of year when not much is growing in the natural world. The fields are cold and empty, and not much besides the heartiest of plants can survive.

However, this bleakness doesn't last—since the beginning of time, this period of dark and cold has always been followed by sunnier, livelier days. But we don't get to those without passing through the winter first. Yule is about honoring this time of darkness as an essential part in the ever-turning wheel of life.

The winter solstice is the perfect time for working magick about banishment. If you've got bad habits you want to drop or painful memories you want to move on from, this is the right holiday to begin that journey.

Although the dates vary from year to year, the winter solstice typically falls somewhere near December 20th.

# Imbolg

Also known as Imbolc or Brigid, this holiday falls on February 1st. At this point in the year, we're still in the throes of winter, but by this time, spring is well on its way! And it's the perfect holiday for meditating on and preparing for this upcoming season of life.

While the winter solstice may be a good time for banishing bad habits, Imbolg is the right time to begin new ones. Similarly, if there are positive things in your life that may have fallen to the wayside, this holiday is the perfect time to rededicate yourself to those things.

Finally, Imbolg is the right time to begin that oh-so-dreaded yearly ritual of spring cleaning. So, spruce up your home altar if you've got one and organize your tools to ensure that everything is in order when those sunnier months roll around...and they'll be here quicker than you might think!

# The Spring Equinox

At the spring (or vernal) equinox, spring is finally here! Like the winter solstice, the exact day will vary from year to year, but it typically falls around March 20th. Astronomically, this is one of the two days on the calendar when daytime and nighttime are completely equal in length.

Spiritually, this is a holiday of new life and the blessings that go along with it. So, pull out any tools that need to be consecrated and seal them with spiritual power at this time.

The spring equinox is also the time when some Wiccans and other Pagans celebrate and honor the goddess Ostara—in some traditions, this holiday is named after her. Ostara is depicted as a young, beautiful maiden, which is fitting, since at this time of year the earth is in the same condition. She, like the holiday, represents newness, innocence and purity, which is why I recommend blessing rituals at this time.

Flowers and other beautiful signs of life are a must for the equinox, so don't be afraid to fill your home to the gills with these symbols of regeneration.

# Beltane

Falling on April 30th or May 1st, Beltane (or May Day) is another occasion to surround yourself with plenty of beautiful flowers and other plants. However, this is a holiday that is also specifically associated with fertility.

But before you go out and buy a basinet, keep in mind that fertility can be about more than just childbirth. This is the time of year when the ground is at its most fertile, and many crops are planted on or around Beltane. Even if you don't have much of a green thumb yourself, it's the perfect holiday to honor the earth and the life-giving bounty that she is about to provide for us.

# The Summer Solstice

The summer solstice (aka Midsummer or Litha) is the polar opposite of the winter solstice. This is the day when the sun is at the peak of its powers—daylight is longest, while nighttime is shortest.

Because of this association with the sun, we honor it and the God (which corresponds to it) at this time. Be sure to honor him with a gift of flowers or other plants to show your appreciation for his life-giving light.

This is also the holiday when Wiccans are the most likely to get a little wild and crazy. We want to honor and respect the sun at this holiday, but there's no reason that it can't be done with a little joyful partying!

The summer solstice date will vary, but it falls somewhere around June 20th each year.

# Lammas

Lammas (also known as Lughnasadah) is a late-summer festival that falls on August 1st. And it can be downright frightening.

In the olden days, crops were not quite ready to harvest at this point in the year, but they were well on their way. Even if things looked promising, farmers always had the fear in the back of their minds that it wouldn't be enough to keep their families afloat during the cold winter months.

However, instead of running from their fears, they created an entire holiday about them! Similarly, Lammas is a good time for you to face your own fears. Is there something you've been putting off this year? Now is the time to begin! Is there something in your life that frightens you? Bring it out into the open on Lammas to deprive it of its power!

There are lots of things to be scared of in this world, but when we set aside time like this to face them head on with a clear mind, we actually get the upper hand over them.

# The Autumn Equinox

Like the spring equinox, the autumn equinox (or Mabon) is a time of balance. Once again on this day, light and darkness come in equal measure. However, unlike in the spring, we approach this holiday knowing that the sun is in its decline and close to being replaced by the darkness of winter. But once again, we honor this time of year as essential to the never-ending cycle of life.

Mabon is a time for giving thanks—for a successful harvest, for friends and family, for the beautiful changing colors of the leaves, and everything in between. If you have anything in your life that you're grateful for, the autumn equinox is the time to make your thanks known.

The date of this holiday varies, but it will fall each year sometime close to September 20th.

# Samhain

The rest of the world may know it as Halloween, but for Wiccans, October 31st will always be Samhain.

While there's nothing wrong with having fun with ghosts, goblins, jack-o-lanterns, and plenty of candy, this holiday is actually of the utmost importance for witches.

By Didi Clarke

It is the point in the year when we give honor to loved ones who are no longer here with us. Death is a natural part of life, and on Samhain, we remember those who have completed their life's journey before us.

Visiting the graves of loved ones or burning a candle in their memory are two common ways that Wiccans commemorate the dead, but even if that's not possible, simply taking some time on this day to reminisce and think of good times gone by can bring honor to your departed friends or family members.

Samhain is also the time of year when the natural world and the spiritual world are in closest communion. Many witches take advantage of this fact by using this time for magick that involves spirits of the dead or other spiritual beings.

# CHAPTER 7: TYPES OF MAGICK

From the get go, I've tried to make it abundantly clear that Wicca is a diverse and varied religion. Because we have no central authority or universally accepted creeds, countless different magickal practices and philosophies have emerged—some popular, some known only by their creators; some that exist harmoniously, and some that are irreconcilably different. And it's this freedom and creativity that drew me to Wicca in the first place.

In this chapter, I'm going to attempt to give you an overview of some of the major traditions and niches in the world of Wicca. This is by no means an exhaustive list of different types of magick—I'm highly skeptical that such a thing could even be compiled—but it will give you a good cross-section of the types of magick that are being performed.

I'm sure that as you go deeper in your own personal practice, certain types of magick will begin to appeal to you more than others. This is perfectly normal and acceptable. There's something to be said for people who can focus their time and attention in order to become an expert specialist. However, when you're starting out with Wicca, it's important to keep an open mind about everything that's out there. What seems uninteresting at first glance can often become a lifelong passion the more you explore it!

By Didi Clarke

# Green Witchcraft

Green witchcraft, plant magick, herbal magick—these are all terms that refer to magick that focuses on the natural world. Green witches use all sorts of flowers, herbs, and other living things to work their will and harness spiritual energy.

There's no requirement that you have to be a gardener if you want to practice plant magick, but many witches find themselves doing just that as they gain experience in the craft. There's no one pickier or more fickle about where their supplies come from than a green witch—and I say that 100% from personal experience!

However, green witchcraft is not just about keeping your magickal spice cabinet stocked. It's about developing a deeper relationship with Mother Nature as well. A truly powerful green witch doesn't just take from the earth as she sees fit. She attempts to develop a deep respect for all life on the planet; she attunes her body and mind to the rhythm and cycles of nature. And most importantly she gives back to the earth that has given her so much already.

Since green witchcraft is so nature-based, you'll find plenty of earthy gods and goddesses within this practice too. Gaia, who is personified as our earth mother, is a popular choice, but any deity associated with nature and growth is welcome in the world of plant magick.

If you think that green witchcraft is something you'd like to pursue further, be sure to check out my book *Herbs for Witchcraft*. In it, I take a deeper look at the hows and whys of plant magick.

# White Magick

If you've ever been described as a nurturer or an empath, then white magick should be right up your alley. It's all about tapping into the light and love of the universe in order to spread peace and healing.

White magick actually spans numerous different traditions within Wicca—you can practice white plant magick, white ritual magick, etc. What draws these practices together under the umbrella term of "white magick" is the intent behind them. A white witch seeks to alleviate suffering and cultivate joy.

This type of magick includes "defensive" spells, like spells of banishment or protection, but it also includes more proactive magick too—like blessing rituals or rituals designed to cultivate large amounts of positive spiritual energy. It's a truly broad field of study with the best of intentions behind it.

For those who want to know more about white magick, be sure to check out my book, *The White Magick Spell Book*. You'll find plenty of spells in there for sending lots of love and peace out into the world.

# Black Magick

Although I don't recommend you go down this path, we can't talk about white magick without briefly touching on its polar opposite—black magick.

Whereas white magick aims to help and heal, black magick aims to hurt and destroy. Curses and hexes both fall under the category of black magick, as does any spell that has the intention of increasing suffering in the world.

Some might also put things like demon summoning in the same category, but I'm going to go out on a limb and say that that's not always the case. If you're summoning a demon to do harm to someone else, sure, that's black magick. However, if you're summoning a demon just to see what happens, I'm not so sure. I think that's a pretty stupid plan and highly advise against it, but I think black magick is more defined by the intention behind the spell than the actual components of the spell itself.

# Gray Magick

Gray magick falls somewhere between black and white. It includes things like love spells and money magick.

As it's plain to see, causes like love and money are not as idealistic and noble as those found in white magick.

But on the other hand, they're not downright evil like the things you find in black magick. They're somewhere in the middle, and this means that there's plenty of healthy debate about their appropriateness.

I can't tell you if gray magick is something you should take an interest in—that's something you'll have to decide for yourself. But I bring it up to illustrate again what a diverse, independent spirit you'll find in the world of Wicca. Gray magick is just one thing among many that you'll have to grapple with ethically, and no one but yourself can decide what decision you should make. It can be daunting at times, but it's also wildly liberating.

I've dabbled in gray magick myself, and you can read more about it in my first two books, *Forbidden Wiccan Spells Vol. 1: Magick for Love and Power* and *Forbidden Wiccan Spells Vol. 2: Magick for Wealth and Prosperity*.

# Ritual Magick

If you're like me and have and love all things theatrical, then ritual magick is absolutely for you! It's also great for folks who love to organize and plan. With this type of magick, it's not about doing things the easy way—it's about doing them with flair and symbolism.

In the world of ritual magick, we take very seriously the link between spiritual energy and our spellwork. Within a well-crafted ritual, nothing is left up to chance. Every word, every action, every item used is carefully considered and constructed. It's very much like watching a play unfold on stage.

Some witches prefer more spontaneity in their magick, and that's absolutely fine. But for those who see magick as a sacred drama, ritual magick is the way to go.

You can learn more about the intricacies of ritual magick in my book, *The Ritual Magick Manual*.

# CHAPTER 8: WICCAN TOOLS

Tools are an important part of working magick in the world of Wicca. Even though magick technically operates within the realm of spiritual energy, we use things like tools, symbols, and incantations to help create a tangible link to the physical, material world. Many of the most important tools you'll find in Wicca are used to harness and direct spiritual energy according to your will.

That being said, when you're just getting started with Wicca, there's no good reason to go out and spend a ton of money buying tools. It's perfectly fine to collect them here and there as you progress along this spiritual path—ingenuity and thriftiness are a witch's best friend! Start with one or two and see how they work for you.

## Where to Buy Wiccan Tools

The history and source of a tool can have a noticeable impact on its ability to work magick and direct energy. We Wiccans carefully consider the origins of where our objects come from.

The best source for Wiccan tools is undoubtedly yourself. Anything you can construct or create on your own will be infused with your personal energy. Your desire to walk this spiritual path and your dedication to Wicca will enhance anything you make with your own hands.

Additionally, tools that you can find directly in nature will be spiritually potent too. For example, many witches use unadultered tree branches as wands, and in just a little bit I'll show you how to find and select your own.

For tools that you're unable to make yourself, I recommend finding a spiritually minded craftsman to buy from. There are numerous Wiccans, witches, and Pagans that make their living from carefully and lovingly crafting tools for spellwork. By purchasing from them, you're supporting others who walk the path of Wicca, but you're also ensuring that the tools you use were created with a direct spiritual purpose in mind by someone who knows what they're doing.

For everything else, I say buy it from a store and don't worry about it. Wicca is not about perfection—it's the intention behind your magick that counts. The universe is not going to punish you because you can't afford or find an altar cloth from a master weaver. As long as your tools are properly blessed and cared for, they should still get the job done.

With that out of the way, let's take a look as some of the most essential tools you need to get started performing your own spells.

# Wand

Wands and witches go together like nothing else. Even outside the world of Wicca, a magickal wand is something that most people associate with us.

Within the context of a spell, a wand is primarily used to draw energy into your sacred space. You can use it for everything from creating a barrier of spiritual protection to infusing another object with spiritual energy that you have gathered. Wands are most commonly associated with the element of air, which is the medium through which we use it. By tracing different shapes and making different movements in the space surrounding us, wands can harness and direct different types of energy.

Like I mentioned earlier, wands are a great tool to find out in nature. Many witches prefer oak or rowan wands because of their spiritual correspondences, but I recommend spending some time outside to see which trees speak to you personally.

When choosing a wand, look first for branches that have fallen off a tree naturally. If you can't find a suitable one, it's okay to cut one yourself, but do so with the utmost respect. Thank the tree for its sacrifice and always leave a small gift (like a bowl of water) at its trunk.

# Besom

Like wands, a besom (or broomstick) is another iconic tool associated with witchcraft. Unfortunately, we've yet to master the art of gliding silently across the night sky with one in real life. But that doesn't mean they're not useful within the world of Wicca!

A besom is all about consecration and banishment. Just as it physically sweeps a space clean of any debris, it also clears a space of any residual energy (good or bad) that could interfere with the spellwork you're attempting to do.

While a modern-day broom is perfectly acceptable to use, you can actually create a fairly simple besom of your own with just a few items. A large stick for the handle, smaller twigs for the bristles, and some twine to hold them all together is really all it takes. It may not look like a name-brand broom, but it will sure have some witchy charm!

# Candles

I will admit it—I'm a little candle crazy.

While most Wiccans use them to some extent, you'll have to look pretty carefully to find a spell of mine that doesn't call for at least one! What makes candles such an indispensable part of my magick is their versatility—from banishing to blessing to everything in between, candles can serve almost any purpose within a spell.

Candles also tie into another important aspect of magick—colors. While a black candle helps banish negativity, a white candle draws positive energy in. A gold candle is good for inducing psychic visions, but a silver candle is best for honoring the Triple Goddess. As you move through all the different possible hues, the energy that a candle attracts and reflects moves along with it.

Candles also serve a practical purpose in magick because they emit light. I prefer to work my spells without any electric light sources on, so candles are a must if you're doing anything after sunset.

# Incense

Incense is another item you'll see quite frequently in my spells and rituals. Like I said earlier, the purpose of magickal tools is to link the spiritual and the physical worlds, and this is best done when you engage all five of your senses. We might not immediately associate magick and smell with each other, but it's a powerful sense that shouldn't be neglected!

Incense is a great tool for purification and cleansing, but it's also a must-have for Wiccans that are interested in psychic development and communication with the spirit world.

# Blessing Your Tools

Before using your tools in a spell, they absolutely must be blessed. This process helps rid the objects of negative energy and seals them with your will and intention. There are elaborate rituals you can use for blessing tools, but if you're just getting started, it's okay to go the simple route.

The following blessing ritual only requires a bowl of water that's been sitting outside under the light of a full moon for at least three hours.

To bless your tools, place your right thumb into the bowl of water and then draw a straight line up and down over the object you want to consecrate. As you do this, say the following:

---

*This tool is blessed and sealed for the working of magick. I cleanse it of all negativity and cover it with the pure light and love of the universe. So mote it be.*

---

# CHAPTER 9: SACRED CIRCLES

If you're at all familiar with spells and rituals within Wicca, you may have already heard people talking about the idea of a "sacred circle." The processes of casting (or opening) and closing (or releasing) a sacred circle often acts as a bookend for whatever ritual you're performing—they come at the very beginning and end of a spell.

In this chapter, we're going to be looking at what a sacred circle is, why we use them in Wicca, and how to cast one yourself.

## What Is a Sacred Circle?

Circles are an important symbol, both in and outside of Wicca. They represent a sense of completeness or unity, since they have no defined beginning or end. This simple shape is also a sign of protection or a barrier—since it's created from one continuous line, there are no points in the shape that are weaker than others. This barrier that a circle creates works both ways, too. It keeps things out, but it also keeps things in.

# Why Use a Sacred Circle?

Within Wicca, the concept of a sacred circle encapsulates all of the above meanings. The circle represents unity—of life, of the physical and spiritual worlds, and of humans and divinity.

It also represents protection from outside forces. When you work magick, you allow spiritual to energy to flow into the physical world. Unfortunately, not all spiritual energy and not all spiritual beings are benevolent or want to help you achieve your desired goal. By casting a sacred circle, you protect yourself and your ritual from forces that would like nothing more than to sabotage them.

Finally, the sacred circle is a means of containment. The purpose of magick is to control and focus spiritual energy. By creating a barrier between your sacred space and the "real" world, you help contain the energy you raise so that it can more easily be manipulated according to your will.

In short, sacred circles make your magick more potent than it would otherwise be.

However, casting a sacred circle is not the only way to achieve the goals I've just mentioned. Depending on the particular magickal tradition you're working within, you may discover different ways of protecting yourself and containing the energy you raise.

For example, some witches may prefer to call upon a particular deity for protection when performing a ritual. And others may opt for calling upon the spirits of the cardinal directions (north, south, east, west) or the spirits of the four elements (earth, fire, water, air). And yet others may have practices that incorporate all four of these things.

That being said, if you're just getting started in the world of Wicca and aren't familiar with these diverse practices, casting a sacred circle is a good introduction to the concept of spiritual protection. It can be incorporated into pretty much any spell or ritual you'll encounter.

# How to Cast a Sacred Circle

Casting a sacred circle can be as simple or as complex as you'd like to make it. Some witches choose to physically represent their circle (typically with salt or chalk), but others prefer a more symbolic circle that's felt but not seen.

To begin, clear the area that you'll be performing your ritual in. Whether you physically mark it or not, you need to be able to walk the circumference of your sacred circle without any obstructions.

Traditionally in Wicca, a sacred circle is nine feet in diameter, but if that's not a size that you can practically accommodate, it's only important that the circle be large enough to accommodate you, your supplies, and any actions that the spell or ritual involves.

To begin, stand at the center of your space, close your eyes, and visualize warm, white spiritual light emanating from your heart. Take a few deep breaths and imagine this light as it begins to grow and envelop the space around you. This light is healing, protective energy.

Now, move to the northernmost point of your soon-to-be circle and begin to walk its circumference in a clockwise motion. As you walk, imagine a wall of golden light that begins to erect itself where your feet land on the floor. This is the barrier that will contain the energy you raise within the circle and protect you from negative energy outside of it. You'll want to make three complete rotations around your circle for it to be sealed.

As you make these rotations, repeat the following:

---

*This sacred place is bathed in the light of goodness. May all within this circle be protected by the barrier I raise. I cast this sacred circle by the might of my will.*

---

Once you've made your three rotations, your circle is officially cast and you're ready to move onto the ritual itself!

If at all possible, do not cross the boundary of your sacred circle until your spell is complete. However, I'd be lying if I said I've never forgotten a crucial item outside my circle once or twice in my life! In instances where it's absolutely necessary for you to leave, you'll want to cut a temporary door in the sacred circle. Never just walk through your barrier—as this will decrease its power or eliminate it entirely.

To do this, move to the easternmost point, and with your right index finger, literally trace a rectangle in the air that's large enough for you to move through. And then step through it.

Once you have what you need, return through this space, face towards the door, and repeat the following:

*I re-seal the door that I have opened. The circle is complete once again.*

# How to Close a Sacred Circle

Once you're finished with your spell or ritual, you need to close your sacred circle to allow the energy you've raised to enter into the physical world.

To do this, begin at the southernmost point and walk around it three times—but this time you want to move counterclockwise instead of clockwise.

As you walk, repeat the following:

---

*The sacred circle is now released. May the energy within move into the world and work my will. So mote it be.*

---

(FYI—"so mote it be" is a statement of affirmation within Wicca. It's similar to when Christians use the term "amen.")

# CHAPTER 10: HOW TO CREATE YOUR OWN SPELL

When you're just getting started with Wicca, the idea of creating your own spells and rituals can feel pretty intimidating. However, I think that this process can do wonders for your progress. It's perfectly fine and normal to follow what other folks have written, but there's no better feeling than working through a ritual that you designed and created yourself.

In this chapter, I'm going to walk you through the process of designing a basic ritual with the use of simple format. There's no one right way to do magick, so as your ability to design spells improves, I highly encourage you to deviate from the format I'm going to give you based on your own personal experiences of what works and what doesn't. However, if you're a complete beginner, it's often useful to have a solid starting point.

# Step 1: Determining the Purpose of Your Ritual

You have to have a purpose or intention in mind before you can design a ritual. Sitting down and simply saying to yourself, "I want to write a spell," will rarely yield good results.

So, before you begin, take some time to think about a problem you're facing or a type of magick that you're interested in. The more specific you can be, the better. For example, "I want to create a plant magick spell," is pretty broad—you have a type of magick (and that's a good start!), but there's still no intention.

Try to get as precise as possible, like this: "I want to create a plant magick spell that will help me develop psychic abilities faster."

However, rituals and spells don't have to just be about achieving some specific, practical outcome. You could create a personalized ritual to celebrate a particular holiday or something that honors a particular deity, too. Both of those have a specific intention in mind too.

Once you have your purpose in mind, it's time to move onto step two.

# Step 2: Brainstorming Correspondences

By determining your specific intention at the get-go, it will be easier to decide what tools and symbols you want to use in your ritual.

There are a number of fantastic books and websites that will help you come up with correspondences, but it's also perfectly fine to trust your gut on these and go with what feels right to you. It's more important to have a personal connection with these correspondences than to simply choose things that other people have decided have certain magickal properties.

When choosing correspondences, don't forget to assemble a wide array. Remember, physical objects aren't the only things that have them—colors, symbols, days, months, moon phases, and other concepts like these also make for powerful correspondences.

The goal at this point in the process is to give yourself plenty of options. You won't be using every single correspondence you come up with in your finished ritual, but it's always better to have too many than not enough.

# Step 3: Paring Down Your Correspondences

Once you have your long list of correspondences, it's time to winnow it down to something more manageable.

To use our earlier example of plant magick for increasing psychic abilities, your initial list might look something like this:

- Silver
- Purple
- Lavender
- Dark moon phase
- Mirrors
- Saturdays
- The number six
- The Crone
- Incense
- Cedar
- December

As you can see, there's lots to work with, but we need to reduce them for both practical and spiritual reasons.

On the practical side, that list is simply too much to juggle. Trying to pinpoint a dark moon that falls on a Saturday in December will mean that it could be years before you'll find a day to perform your spell! Spiritually, I find that spells and rituals that are tightly focused perform much better than those with a ton of disparate elements.

So, my thinking for narrowing down correspondences in this particular case would go like this:

*This is supposed to be plant magick, so I definitely want to include lavender. Cedar is an option too, but since lavender is naturally purple, it makes more sense to include it. Choosing lavender also means that I could include incense, since that's a pretty easy scent to find. I'll perform this ritual on a dark moon because it is nice to have a specific day in mind when planning these things. Plus, the dark moon also corresponds with the Crone, which means that I could incorporate a prayer or petition to her.*

Your train of thought might be different from mine, and that's great—go with where your gut leads you! The important thing is that your choices have some sort of internal logic to them.

Now it's time to design the ritual itself!

# Step 4: The Essential Parts of a Ritual

Every ritual should begin with some sort of magickal protection.

Casting a sacred circle like we discussed in the previous chapter will fulfill this requirement, but it's by no means the only way to protect yourself. In my example of a plant magick ritual for psychic abilities, we could open with an invocation to the Crone asking her to bless and protect the magick we're about to perform. What's important is that you have some sort of protective measure in place.

Next, we need to bless the items we're going to use in the ritual. Your multipurpose items (wands, etc.) should have been blessed beforehand, but the ritual-specific ones will need to be consecrated now. You can use the short blessing I showed you at the end of the chapter on tools if you'd like, but if you'd rather craft one specific to your spell, that's fine too.

Now comes the "meat" of your spell. This is the time when the magick happens! As you're designing this section, be as specific as possible (and always write everything down!)—you want to be able to accurately repeat these steps when the real time comes!

It's challenging to say exactly what you need to include, because it can vary so much depending on your intention and the tools you're using. My advice is to be creative, but don't be afraid to mimic what you've seen in other spells—in this book and beyond.

To continue my example, I would invoke the Crone here as I walked around the room six times with the burning incense, asking her to bless me with her wisdom every time I worked on my psychic abilities in this place.

Finally comes the concluding material of your ritual. This is the time when you thank and release any deities or spirits you may have called upon and close your sacred circle, if you opened one.

Creating a ritual may seem daunting at first, especially if you don't have any previous experience with Wicca. My suggestion is to read as many spells and rituals from different sources as you can find. The more you learn about them, the more natural their rhythm and logic will become to you.

Keep being creative and keep testing the spells you design—experience is the best teacher you'll ever find!

By Didi Clarke

# CHAPTER 11: SOLITARY WITCH INITIATION SPELL

When Wiccans join a coven, it's an important affair. Becoming a part of the larger group is a big decision—for both the initiate and the coven itself. This process of initiation is typically not a one-time thing. The entire process can span a matter of weeks or even months before the initiation is made official. And the whole thing is usually topped off with a magickal ritual officially welcoming the new member into the group.

Even though you might not be part of a *traditional* coven, a solitary witch is still a part of something larger than herself—she's part of the worldwide group of practitioners who follow the path of Wicca. Even though we might be diverse in our beliefs and far away from one another, our desire to connect with and harness the energy of the universe unites us on a spiritual level.

And that is something worth celebrating and commemorating.

In this chapter, I'm going to show you an initiation spell that will help you officially mark your entrance into the world of Wicca. You may be taking a solitary path, but the love and goodwill of Wiccans everywhere still surrounds you, and this ritual is a way to tap into that good energy.

# Preparing for Initiation

The decision to officially step into the world of Wicca is not one you should take lightly. Just like deciding to join a coven would require careful thought and consideration, this is something you should spend some time really thinking about.

There's nothing wrong with staying a curious spiritual seeker, and there's nothing wrong with practicing magick without an official initiation. This is a ritual meant for people who are certain that Wicca is the religion they want to pursue. So don't rush into this whole process too quickly.

Traditionally, an initiate would be required to study and practice for a year and a day before being admitted into a coven. There's no rule that says you have to wait that long for a solitary initiation, but I bring this tradition up to emphasize the fact that Wicca is not something you should adopt on a fleeting whim.

Give yourself plenty of time to really consider the decision you're making. If you have open-minded and spiritual people in your life, talk it over with them and seek their advice on the issue. Spend time meditating in nature to see what the universe has to say about the matter. If you're inclined to pray, ask the God and Goddess for their divine guidance.

Once you've decided that this is the path you want to pursue and that it's time to self-initiate, I highly recommend reading (and re-reading!) this ritual all the way through. Practice the words and motions, so that they feel natural and familiar to you. We all have a tendency to rush through the preparation part of magick (because the magick itself is so exciting and fun), but this is one spell you don't want to mess up or stumble through. Collect your items and prepare your ritual space in advance so that everything can go as smoothly and perfectly as possible.

# Performing the Solitary Witch Initiation Ritual

You'll need the following items for this spell:
- 1 silver (or white) candle
- 1 gold (or yellow) candle
- Matches or a lighter
- 1 purple ribbon (long enough to tie around your wrist)
- Incense and holder (pick a fragrance you love)
- 1 bowl of water
- 1 handheld bell

Begin the ritual in the center of your space while holding your bell.

Ring it loudly four times and repeat this:

*I summon the spirits of the four cardinal directions into this sacred space. Bear witness to the commitment I make.*

Place the bell down and move to the northernmost point of your space.

With your hands raised above your head, say the following:

*Spirits of the north, I welcome you. Your presence gives me wisdom.*

Now, move to the east and (with your hands raised again) say this:

*Spirits of the east, I welcome you. Your presence gives me courage.*

Next, move to the south and say this:

*Spirits of the south, I welcome you. Your presence gives me strength.*

Finally, move to the west and say this:

*Spirits of the west, I welcome you. Your presence gives me hope.*

Return to the center of your space and pick up the incense. Carefully light it and allow it to begin smoking. When it's ready, return again to the northernmost point and slowly begin walking a clockwise circle around your space.

As you walk, repeat this three times:

*I bless and consecrate this space with the element of air. All spirits of goodwill are welcome to enter the circle and lend their light.*

By Didi Clarke

Once again, return to the center of your space and put down the incense. You won't need it anymore during the ritual, but you should allow it to continue smoking.

Next, arrange your candles in the center of your space, so that the gold one is on the left and the silver one is on the right. These represent the Lord and Lady of Wicca—gold for the God (whose symbol is the sun) and silver for the Goddess (whose symbol is the moon).

Light the gold candle and repeat the following as you raise your hands above your head:

*I call upon the power of the great God, our solar father. Lend your warmth and guiding light as I begin my journey on the path of Wicca.*

Now, light the silver candle and repeat the following as you raise your hands above your head:

*I call upon the power of the great Goddess, our lunar mother. Lend your wisdom and love as I begin my journey on the path of Wicca.*

Next, take your bowl of water and hold it over the flames of these candles—be careful not to burn yourself!

As you hold the bowl, repeat this blessing:

*This water is filled with the light of the great Lord and Lady. May their blessings fall upon all whom it touches.*

Place the bowl back down and dip your right thumb in it. Now, take your thumb and carefully draw a circle of water on your forehead. You should move your thumb in a clockwise motion (relative to you).

Once this is complete, say:

*I am sealed with the power of the Divine. I am safe on my journey.*

Finally, take your purple ribbon and tie it around your right wrist.

Then, say the following:

*I set my will and seal my intention with this ribbon. I bind myself to the love of Wicca. I cannot know what the future will bring, but I know that the love and divine goodness of the universe urges me on deeper into my spiritual practice. I commit myself to the sacred way, no matter where it may lead me.*

To end the ritual, extinguish your candles and your incense (if it is still burning).

Once the initiation is over, you should dispose of your water by pouring it directly on the ground outside. Your candles should be disposed of respectfully—don't use them again. However, you should keep your ribbon as a reminder of the commitment you made here today. You don't have to wear it 24/7, but do keep it in a safe special place.

Finally, let me be the first to give you an official welcome into the world of Wicca!

# CHAPTER 12: BLESSING SPELL

In the chapter on Wiccan tools, we looked at a quick, easy blessing spells for getting started with your sacred objects. In this chapter, I'm going to show you a blessing ritual that's a bit more complex and in-depth. It can be used as a substitute for the earlier spell, but it can also be used for a number of different purposes aside from consecrating objects.

## The Purpose of a Blessing Spell

Blessings spells serve two purposes—similar to how our sacred circles serve two purposes.

The first is to rid an object or person of any negative energy that they may have surrounding them. It's important to note that someone or something doesn't have to be cursed or evil to accumulate bad energy. Unfortunately, negative energy can cling to us simply by existing out in the real world.

From an angry boss to a nosy neighbor, we're forced to confront unpleasant people and situations on an almost daily basis. These interactions, while not devastatingly bad when taken individually, add up over time, and they affect us on more than just a spiritual level.

Who hasn't experienced something like this—a flat tire or other minor annoyance in the morning puts us in a bad mood and sets a negative tone for the day, and as the day progresses, our anger or sadness grows (sometimes imperceptibly) until we're a sulking, fuming mess by the time the sun sets!

Blessing spells help wash away all that accumulated negativity so that we're left with a fresh, clean slate. And this is important for objects too! Even though they may be inanimate, bad energy certainly clings to them as well, which can then be transferred to yourself or others.

Secondly, a blessing spell imbibes a person or thing with positive, healing energy too. It's not enough to just wash away the bad—you want to add something good in its place! And a blessing does just that.

This particular blessing spell I'm going to show you is meant to be an all-purpose ritual that you can turn to in a number of different situations. From consecrating your tools to blessing a new home to blessing a loved one before they embark on a long journey, it's designed to be applicable for a wide range of things.

Within the ritual, we'll be invoking the Triple Goddess—and specifically, we'll be invoking the Maiden aspect of the Goddess. If you'll recall, she is associated with purity and newness, which is just what we need for a blessing.

# Performing the Blessing Spell

To successfully perform this spell, you'll need the following items:
- 1 new bundle of sage (for banishing negativity)
- 1 silver (or white) candle (to represent the Goddess)
- 1 pink rose (which will act as a magick wand)
- Whatever is to be blessed (note: if you're blessing a home or other large place, choose a meaningful object to represent it)
- Matches or a lighter

To begin your ritual, cast a scared circle like I taught you in chapter nine of this book.

Once your circle is cast, return to the center and light your silver (or white) candle.

After it is lit, raise your hands above your head and repeat the following:

---

*Holy Goddess, fair Maiden, be present in this sacred place. Send your divine light that it may be a blessed gift of purification. I thank you for your power. So mote it be.*

---

Now, pick up your sage and carefully light it. Allow it to develop a healthy burn until it's smoking steadily. If you're blessing an object, move the sage over it from right to left three times. If you're blessing a person, walk a counterclockwise circle around them three times while holding the sage. If you're blessing a space, walking the perimeter of your sacred circle three times clockwise while holding the sage.

As you do that, repeat this phrase three times:

---

*I banish negativity and ill will. By the presence of this sacred smoke, all bad energy must depart. This object/person/place is cleansed of what hinders it/them.*

---

Carefully place your sage down somewhere where it can continue to smoke but will not pose a fire hazard.

Now, pick up your pink rose and hold it in your right hand like a wand—but watch out for the thorns! While standing in front of the object or person, slowly trace a five-pointed star surrounded by a circle in the air. Your circle should begin at the top point of the star and move clockwise. If you're blessing a space, move to the northernmost point of your sacred circle to draw the pentagram.

As you trace this shape in the air, repeat this blessing:

*The goodness and light of the great Maiden is in this place. May it leave nothing untouched. Sweet Maiden, I call upon you to bless and purify this object/person/place. May your watchful eye and caring grace never leave it/them.*

To finalize this blessing, walk three times clockwise around your sacred circle while saying this:

*My intention is set and the blessing is sealed. Let no powers undo what my will has made. So mote it be.*

Before you end the ritual entirely, you need to thank and release the Goddess.

To do this, repeat the following farewell to the Maiden:

*Great Goddess of the moon, your presence has been felt and appreciated. Though we depart this sacred circle, bind our hearts to yours, that we may be as one. So mote it be.*

Extinguish your candle immediately following this. If your sage is still smoking, you should extinguish it completely now as well.

To finish up your ritual, simply close the sacred circle that you opened at the beginning. Your blessing is now completely and fully active!

# CHAPTER 13: GOOD LUCK SPELL

I think most people would agree that we could all use a little more good luck in our lives, and that's what this spell intends to help you with! Whether you feel like nothing is going right at the moment or you've built up a solid streak of living the good life that you want to keep going, this ritual is meant to surround you with positive vibes and a pinch of luck.

Now, it's important not to blow the concept of "good luck" out of proportion. This spell makes no guarantees about helping you win the lottery or falling madly in love by this time tomorrow. Good luck is a bit more nebulous than that. Luck is about happy accidents and unexpected small things that make your day a little brighter. And luck works best when you don't have a predefined goal in mind—the universe is ready and waiting to surprise you if you allow yourself to be open to its possibilities!

## Performing the Good Luck Ritual

This ritual, if at all possible, should be performed on the night a full moon. This particular moon phase is associated with serendipity and abundance, so it's a good fit for this type of ritual. If you can't wrangle this specific time, don't let it discourage you from trying out the spell anyways—it's just that you might see enhanced results during a full moon.

The items you'll need for the good luck spell include:

- 1 bundle of mint sprigs (should be enough to create a small circle with the sprigs)
- 1 blue-colored gem or stone (color is more important that type in this instance, and this should also be small enough to fit in a pocket or purse)
- 1 gold or yellow candle
- Matches or a lighter

To begin, you'll want to cast your sacred circle as described in chapter nine. There's not much movement or physical action in this spell, so you won't need a ton of space to perform it.

Start by lighting your yellow candle and repeating this:

*Spirits of fortune and luck be with me in this place. Lend your merry light that it may shine upon me.*

Next, you're going to want to create a small circle with your mint sprigs. It doesn't have to be geometrically perfect, but make sure there aren't any major holes or cracks in the ring. Place your yellow candle at the northernmost point of this ring.

Now, you should say this:

*I cast this circle with lucky herbs from the earth. May their power mingle with the spirits of fortune that fill the air.*

Place your blue stone at the center of your mint ring. This will act as the talisman that will draw luck and positive energy towards you.

Once it is in place, say this:

---

*I charge this stone with the power of luck. When I hold it close, may good fortune always be nearby. Spirits and herb, lend me your energies. I ask for luck, so mote it be.*

---

To conclude, collect your mint, extinguish your candle, and close your sacred circle.

Your blue stone is now charged to help you attract luck and serendipity. You can carry it around with you as you go about your day, or, if that's not possible, leave it in your bedroom or living room to still experience its effects. However, the power of luck is not permanent—you'll need to re-charge your stone once every three months with this ritual if you want to experience continued effects from it.

# CHAPTER 14: LIVING THE LIFE OF A SOLITARY WITCH

B y now you should be familiar with all the basics necessary to continue your journey as a solitary witch. There's always more to be learned in the world of Wicca, but I hope that what you've read has given you a clear path and a desire to move deeper into the exciting world of witchcraft.

Being a solitary witch can seem a little bit lonesome at times, but I think that you'll find it's equally empowering to set out on this journey all on your own. You're in control of where this road takes you, and that freedom is something that not everyone gets to experience. And always remember this—you're never truly alone. There are countless other seekers making the same journey as you, and that is a spiritual connection that's just as strong as any physical one.

And who could forget the great God and Goddess of Wicca? They are our divine teachers, parents, friends, and companions. With them by your side, the path is never empty, and your possibilities are wide open.

I invite you to investigate my new website, ExploreWicca.com. It's full of long-form, original spells and articles meant to instruct and enrich you spiritually. And best of all, the content you'll find there is absolutely free. Stop by today—I love having new visitors!

Finally, I would be extremely grateful for an honest review of the book. I want to provide my readers with spells and magickal rituals that are important and useful to them, and receiving your feedback is one way I can better serve you.

Blessed Be,

Didi

# CHAPTER 15: READ MORE FROM DIDI CLARKE

## Herbs for Witchcraft: The Green Witches' Grimoire of Plant Magick

*Welcome to the world of the green witch—where nature and magick meet!*

Plants are a life-giving source of power for every witch. In *Herbs for Witchcraft*, you'll find everything you need to become adept at harnessing this power! The world of plant magick is one of the oldest and most exciting branches of witchcraft—and you too can learn this ancient art!

*What You'll Find*

This book serves as your guide to all things plant magick. From learning what herbs are best for certain purposes to planning spells based on the season, *Herbs for Witchcraft* takes you through everything you need to get started in the world of green witchcraft. All of these spells and rituals are 100% original and come from Didi Clarke's firsthand experience with the magick of plants.

In particular, you'll discover:

- Plant-based spells and rituals
- Plant folklore
- The beliefs of green witchcraft
- Nature-based Gods and Goddesses
- How to communicate with the natural world
- And much more!

*Are you ready to explore the wonder and power of the natural world?*

*Herbs for Witchcraft* is your complete guidebook to the art of plant magick—it's the perfect pick for witches and other spiritual seekers looking to get closer to nature! Buy it today and begin your journey!

# Forbidden Wiccan Spells: Magick for Love and Power (Vol. 1)

Enchant your way to romance with these Wiccan love spells! Become a master of power magick! Learn all this and much more with this original spell book from Didi Clarke!

Whether you're trying to seduce that special someone or want to show others who's the boss, *Forbidden Wiccan Spells: Magick for Love and Power* has something for everyone. With each chapter, you'll find authentic Wiccan magic that will help you unlock your dreams in love and life!

*What You'll Find*

Within the pages of *Magick for Love and Power*, you'll find one-of-a-kind spells written and tested by Didi Clarke herself—you won't find books on witchcraft like this anywhere else!

If you're new to Wicca, never fear—this book uses a wicca for beginners approach. The spells are explained thoroughly, and each one comes with a detailed item list and step-by-step directions.

And there's plenty for more experienced witches too. These unique magick rituals will enhance your skills and help you tap into the full potential of love and power! In this book, you'll find a wide variety of magickal practices to explore, including:
- Herbal Magick
- Candle Magick
- Mantra Magick
- Elemental Magick

*Are you ready to spice up your life with love spells?*

Love is a powerful force, and when you combine it with the power of witchcraft, the results can be truly magickal! In *Magick for Love and Power*, you'll get access to genuine spells and rituals that will help you attract romance into your life and keep the flames of love burning for years to come!

These love spells include:
- Flame gazing to find your true love
- Mantras to keep your partner faithful
- Potions to repair a damaged relationship
- And much more!

*Are you ready to harness the strength of power magick?*

These power spells are here to change your life for the better. Whether you want to be more assertive at work or tap into the power of the Spirits, this magick will leave you feeling confident and strong!

Here are some of the power spells you'll find in this complete book of witchcraft:
- Amulets for persuasive power
- Rituals for fame
- Incantations for dominance
- Many more!

*Learn the Art of Love Magick and Power Magick Today!*

Unlock the secrets of witchcraft within the pages of this Wiccan book of shadows written for those seeking love and power! If you're ready to take control and live your best life, read *Magick for Love and Power* today!

# Forbidden Wiccan Spells: Magick for Wealth and Prosperity (Vol. 2)

Find true prosperity with these original money spells from Didi Clarke!

Are you ready to embrace the bounty of the Spirit world? Then this is the book for you! *Forbidden Wiccan Spells: Magick for Wealth and Prosperity* lays out everything you need to know in order to master the art of prosperity magick.

*What You'll Find*

Within the pages of *FWS: Magick for Wealth and Prosperity*, you'll find never-before-seen money spells that will help put you on the right track for financial success. From herbal magick to incantations, the rituals in this book teach you a wide variety of Wiccan magick—it's perfect for everyone from the complete beginner to the seasoned witch!

These spells include:

- A fire incantation for financial windfall
- An herbal sachet for business success
- Mantras for material prosperity
- Crystal blessings for attracting wealthy people
- And much more!

*Are You Ready to Transform Your Life With Money Magick?*

These spells won't make you a millionaire overnight—nothing can do that—but that doesn't mean you can't seek help from the Spirit world for money matters! This misunderstood but incredibly effective branch of magick has helped countless witches, Wiccans, and other spiritually minded people take charge of their finances in amazing ways.

*Explore These Powerful Spells Today!*

Each of these rituals has been written and tested by Didi Clarke herself. They're presented in an easy-to-read, step-by-step format and include a detailed item list and suggestions for achieving maximum potency. What are you waiting for? Embrace the wealth of the Universe today with *FWS: Magick for Wealth and Prosperity*!

# Forbidden Wiccan Spells: Dark Goddess Magick (Vol. 3)

Darkness isn't a place of evil—it's a creative force for good that empowers Wiccans and Witches just like you! If you want to learn never-before-seen invocations, spells, and rituals that honor powerful Goddesses, this is the book for you!

*Forbidden Wiccan Spells: Dark Goddess Magick* explores the many Goddesses associated with darkness—Goddesses of the moon, of sleep, of dreams, and yes, even of death. For too long, those afraid of divine feminine power have told us that these Goddesses are "demons" or "monsters" or practitioners of "black magick." But Didi Clarke is here to set the record straight. These divine beings are powerful allies for any witch that approaches them with a clean heart and pure will.

Within the pages of *FWS: Dark Goddess Magick*, you'll find twelve completely original invocations that have been written and performed by Didi herself. In addition to popular Goddesses like Hecate (Goddess of the dead) and Freyja (Goddess of war), you'll find rituals involving lesser-known dark Goddesses like:

- Breksta (Goddess of dreams)
- Oya (Goddess of storms)
- Selene (Goddess of the moon)
- And many more!

Each chapter provides an easy-to-understand history of a particular Goddess, as well as correspondences associated with her. Next, you'll find an item list and step-by-step instructions for a ritual invoking one of these powerful beings. These rituals touch on many different elements of the Craft and include:

- Protection of your home
- Prophetic dreams
- Developing magickal abilities
- Communing with the dead
- Wiccan candle magick
- Wiccan herb magick
- Wiccan crystal magick
- Much more!

Whether you're looking for a book about Wicca for beginners or are a seasoned witch, whether you're a solitary witch or work with a coven, FWS: Dark Goddess

Magick has something for you. It's a great addition to your spell book or your book of shadows! Embrace the power of the dark Goddess within and read it today!

# Forbidden Wiccan Spells: Tarot Cards and Psychic Development Rituals (Vol. 4)

Are you ready to master the skills it takes to become a world-class tarot card reader? Are you looking for proven rituals and techniques that will enhance your psychic development?

*Forbidden Wiccan Spells: Tarot Cards and Psychic Development Rituals* has the answers you're looking for!

Psychic development and the art divination are two of the most misunderstood Spiritual practices out there. But despite the stereotypes, these tools are used every day by rational, ordinary people trying to make better decisions and improve their lives.

In this book, Didi Clarke provides you with everything you need to start transforming your own life with the wisdom of the psychic realm!

*What You'll Find*

Within the pages of *FWS: Tarot Cards and Psychic Development Rituals*, you'll find a comprehensive breakdown of everything you need to become a confident, insightful tarot card reader. From card meanings to developing your own reading style, this book is perfect for beginners or experienced readers who want a refresher course.

In addition to this tarot handbook, you'll also find completely original spells and rituals meant to enhance your psychic abilities. Whether you want to get better at dream interpretation, reading tea leaves, or anything between, these magickal rituals will help you harness the power of the Spirit world to reach that goal!

*Unlock The Future With Tarot Card Readings*

Tarot cards are by far one of the most popular forms of divination available. Unfortunately, becoming a proficient reader can seem like an uphill battle—but it doesn't have to be like that!

Within the pages of *FWS: Tarot Cards and Psychic Development Rituals*, Didi Clarke addresses the most important things every tarot card reader needs to know, including:

- Card meanings for all 78 cards
- Major themes of the four minor arcana suits
- Choosing the right card spread
- Memorizing meanings vs. intuitive reading
- Identifying relationships and themes across cards

*Hone Your Divination Skills With Psychic Development*

Tarot is a fantastic tool, but there is so much more to explore in the world of divination too!

If you're ready to expand your psychic abilities in more ways than one, these spells and rituals should leave you feeling insightful and powerful. The rituals include:

- Invoking Gods of prophecy
- Herbal magick to aid dream interpretation
- Automatic writing
- Meditation for encountering spirit guides
- Candle magick for finding lost objects

*Achieve Your Full Spiritual Potential Today!*

If you're ready to unlock the secrets of the Spirit world through divination of any kind, the time is now! *FWS: Tarot Cards and Psychic Development Rituals* has all the tools you need to become the master of your own life. Read it today!

By Didi Clarke

*Don't forget to sign up for my mailing list and receive your free color magick correspondence chart by following the link below!*

*https://mailchi.mp/01863952b9ff/didi-clarke-mailing-list*

*Find me on Twitter at* @AuthorDidi
*And be sure to like my* Facebok page: facebook.com/authordidiclarke
*You can contact me via email at* authordidiclarke@gmail.com

Made in the USA
Coppell, TX
12 March 2021